Amazing, Crazy and

Bugs and Insects

TJ Rob

Amazing, Crazy and Weird BUGS AND INSECTS
By TJ Rob

Amazing, Crazy and Weird Animal Facts — Volume 3

Copyright Text TJ Rob, 2016
All rights reserved. No part of the book may be reproduced in any form without permission in writing from the author. Reviewers may quote brief passages in review.
ISBN 978-1-988695-39-6

Disclaimer:
No part of this book may be reproduced in any form or by any means, mechanical or electronic, including photocopying or recording, or by an information storage and retrieval system, or transmitted by email without permission in writing from the publisher. This book is for entertainment purposes only. The views expressed are those of author alone.

Published by:
TJ Rob
Suite 609
440-10816 Macleod Trail SE
Calgary, AB T2J 5N8 www.TJRob.com

Photo Credits: Images used under license from Flickr.com, Public Domain, Wikimedia Commons: Cover page, Benjamint444 CC BY-SA 3.0 / Wikimedia Commons; Back Page, Public Domain; pg. 1, Shyamal (L. Shyamal) CC BY-SA 2.5 / Wikimedia Commons; pg. 4, Robert CC BY 3.0 / Wikimedia Commons; pg. 5, jacinta lluch valero / Flickr.com; pg. 6, alljengi / Flickr.com; pg. 7, Cory Doctorow / Flickr.com; pg. 8, Eddy Van 3000 / Flickr.com; pg. 9, Scott Wylie CC BY 2.0 / Wikimedia Commons; pg. 10, Fir002 CC BY-SA 3.0 / Wikimedia Commons ; pg. 11, Fir0002 CC BY-SA 3.0, / Wikimedia Commons; pg. 12, Frank Vassen / Flickr.com; pg. 13, Axel Strauß CC BY-SA 3.0 / Wikimedia Commons; pg. 14, Marshal Hedin / Flickr.com; pg. 15, Marshal Hedin / Flickr.com; pg. 16, Mike Keeling / Flickr.com; pg. 18, Graham Wise CC BY 2.0 / Wikimedia Commons; pg. 19, Mario Solera / Flickr.com; pg. 20, Bernard DUPONT / Flickr.com; pg. 21, Udo Schmidt CC BY-SA 2.0 / Wikimedia Commons; pg. 22, gbohne CC BY-SA 2.0 / Wikimedia Commons; pg. 23, gbohne CC BY-SA 2.0 / Wikimedia Commons; pg. 24, Public Domain; pg. 25, Public Domain; pg. 26, Gail Hampshire / Flickr.com; pg. 26, Gail Hampshire / Flickr.com; pg. 27, Gail Hampshire / Flickr.com; pg. 28, NechakoRiver / Flickr.com; pg. 30, Jeanie J / Flickr.com; pg. 31, Nicolas Gent / Flickr.com; pg. 32, Terry Priest / Flickr.com; pg. 32, Art Farmer CC BY-SA 2.0 / Wikimedia Commons; pg. 32, Zhang Junhong / Flickr.com; pg. 33, Sam Weng / Flickr.com; pg. 34, orestART / Flickr.com; pg. 34, Katja Schulz / Flickr.com; pg. 35, Katja Schulz / Flickr.com; pg. 36, Sarah Zukoff / Flickr.com; pg. 36, Astrobradleyderivative work B kimmel / Public Domain; pg. 38, Ingi Agnarsson, Matjaž Kuntner, Todd A. Blackledge CC BY 2.5 / Wikimedia Commons; pg. 39, EOL Learning and Education Group / Flickr.com; pg. 39, By GalliasM / via Wikimedia Commons

TABLE OF CONTENTS	Page
Let's Explore the World of Bugs	4
Are Bugs and Insects the same thing?	5
That's a Big Bug — The Atlas Moth	6
The See Through Bug — The Glasswing Butterfly	9
The World's Longest Bug — The Borneo Walking Stick	10
That's a LONG Neck — The Giraffe Weevil	13
Hiding in Front of You — Thorn Bugs	14
7 STRANGE BUT TRUE BUG FACTS	17
The Most Painful Bite — The Bullet Ant	18
The Strongest Bug — The Dung Beetle	21
The Ninja Bug — The Assassin Bug	22
Weird and Colorful — The Spiny Flower Mantis	25
Dangerous with a Cute Face — The Puss Moth Caterpillar	26
7 MORE STRANGE BUT TRUE BUG FACTS	29
The Champion Hunter — Dragonflies	30
I Glow in the Dark — Fireflies	33
The "You Can't Miss Me" Bug — The Striped Shieldbug	34
The Giant Killer — The Tarantula Hawk Wasp	37
The Super Web Spinner — Darwin's Bark Spider	38
Please leave a review and Other EXCITING books by TJ Rob	40

Let's Explore the World of Bugs...

Nature is full of wonders.

More than half of all organisms on Earth are Insects.

There are more than one million different species of Insects on the planet.

With so many different Insects on Earth, some Insects look pretty weird. Some Insects do strange things. Some are so creepy that you may want to forget that you ever found out about them!

Here are just some of the weird and wonderful Insects and Bugs that I found interesting.

You may know even more!

Are Bugs and Insects the same thing?

All Bugs are Insects, but not all Insects are bugs. Beetles are not true Bugs, nor are Butterflies or Bees or Flies.

We have just got used to calling a Bug an Insect and an Insect a Bug!

A true Bug is a type of Insect that has a mouth shaped like a straw.

Most true Bugs use their mouths to pierce plants and drink their sap or other juices. Other true Bugs use their piercing mouthparts to eat a variety of Insects, Spiders, and other small animals.

So all true Bugs are Insects, but not all Insects are true Bugs.

That's a Big Bug!
The Atlas Moth

Wing tip looks like the head of a Cobra

The Atlas Moth is one of the biggest Moths on the planet. A female Atlas Moth can measure 11 inches from wing tip to wing tip.

To protect itself from predators, it disguises its wings to resemble the head of a poisonous snake.

Decorated with patterns and markings, the tips of the Atlas Moth's wings look like the shape of a cobra's head.

When the Atlas Moth is threatened, it drops to the ground and fans its huge wings, making a movement that also looks similar to the snake's head and neck.

THEY HAVE NO MOUTHS

Atlas Moth adults don't ever eat. Like many types of moths, they don't even have mouths.

THE COCOONS ARE USED AS PURSES

The cocoons of Atlas Moths are very strong. They are spun from broken strands of brown silk called fagara. The cocoons are collected and made into useable products, including small purses. Some cocoons can be used "as found" by simply installing a zipper!

A VERY SHORT LIFESPAN

After spending about a month in their cocoons, Atlas Moths emerge as adults. As adults their only purpose is to fly around and find a mate.

They live off the stores of energy built up as caterpillars to get them through this period. This only takes about two weeks. Once they breed, and the females lay eggs, they die.

8

The See Through Bug!
The Glasswing Butterfly

This Butterfly's wings are almost completely transparent. You can see right through them.

The only way that you can tell that it has wings at all are the dark borders around the wings. Without these borders, the wings of the Glasswing would be close to invisible to humans.

Most other butterflies have colored patterns on their wings. They use these patterns to scare off predators. The Glasswing Butterfly has another way of doing this entirely. It uses its transparent wings to hide itself from predators, rather than to warn them off.

Glasswings can be found mostly from Central to South America.

The World's Longest Bug!
The Borneo Walking Stick

The Borneo Walking Stick is an insect found in Borneo. They are the world's longest insects, measuring up to 22 inches (56 cm) long.

These Stick insects can live up to three years. They are green, brown or grey in color. The head is the smallest part of the body.

The insect is protected because of its color and shape, which acts like camouflage. It looks like a twig and part of the plant which helps it to hide from birds and other predators. It can even sway in the wind like a twig on the plant that it is resting on.

The Borneo Walking Stick is a plant eater (Herbivore) and only eats at night because that's the time when most of its enemy go to sleep. When the Borneo Walking Stick is attacked it plays dead.

11

12

That's a LONG Neck!
The Giraffe Weevil

The Giraffe Weevil is an insect found on the island of Madagascar, off the east coast of Africa. Very little is known about the Giraffe Weevil. It was only recently discovered in 2008.

This weird looking insect gets the name from its very long neck. Its neck is 3 times longer in the male than the female. When they are looking for a mate, the males use their long necks to fight each other.

Giraffe Weevils grow to only about 1 inch long. They don't bite because they only eat leaves.

The adults feed on the Giraffe Beetle Tree and they spend most of their lives on these trees.

The female lays a single egg on a leaf and then rolls the egg up in the leaf. This gives the unborn baby both protection and food to eat when it hatches.

Hiding in Front of You!
Thorn Bugs

Thorn Bugs have large skeletal plates which look like thorns on a branch. This helps camouflage them to look like a part of the plant they're resting on. It also discourages predators from taking a bite because they're afraid of getting pierced.

Thorn Bugs grow to about half an inch long.

The adult is green or yellow with reddish lines and brownish markings. This species lives in South and Central America, Mexico and Florida.

They live on fruit and ornamental trees. They eat by piercing plant stems with their beaks, and feed upon the sap.

15

16

7 STRANGE BUT TRUE BUG FACTS:

1) Night butterflies have ears on their wings so they can avoid bats.

2) Only about 1% of all insects are harmful to humans. Most insects are harmless, or actually helpful, to humans. For example, without bees to pollinate flowers, plants would not have a way of reproducing and we wouldn't have anything to eat!

3) Locusts can eat their own weight in food in a day. A person eats his own body weight in about 6 months.

4) The earliest fossil cockroach is about 280 million years old — that is 80 million years older than the first dinosaurs!

5) There is only one insect that can turn its head — the praying mantis.

6) The average housefly lives for 1 month.

7) Some male spiders pluck their cobwebs like a guitar. They do this to attract female spiders.

The Most Painful Bite!

The Bullet Ant

The Bullet Ant gets its name from the intense pain you would feel if you were bitten by just 1 of these insects. Anyone getting a bite experiences agonizing and intense pain for the next 12 - 24 hours.

The Bullet Ant is the largest of all ant species in the world. These insects grow up to 1 inch (2.5 cm) long. Because they live in the South American rainforest, most of us will never come across a Bullet Ant.

It is not called the Bullet Ant because they look like a bullet or are faster than a speeding bullet. They get their name because their sting feels like you have just been shot by a bullet.

Have you ever been stung by a wasp or a hornet? Well multiply that pain by 30 and that is what a Bullet Ant sting feels like.

19

20

The Strongest Bug!
The Dung Beetle

Dung Beetles are beetles that eat dung.

Many Dung Beetles roll the dung into round balls which are then either used for food or a breeding chamber. Others bury the dung wherever they find it. A third group just live in manure.

Dung Beetles are the strongest creatures on Earth for their size. No Elephant, or even a Whale, is as strong for its size. Dung Beetles have been measured to lift objects that are more than 1141 times their body weight.

This would be the same as a human weighing 150 pounds moving an object weighing 160,000 pounds.

Dung Beetles have a great sense of direction and can navigate using the Milky Way.

With lots of Dung Beetles going after the same pile of poop, a beetle needs to make a quick getaway once he's rolled his dung ball. But it's not easy to roll a ball of poop in a straight line, especially when you're pushing your ball from behind using your hind legs. So the first thing the dung beetle does is climb on top of his dung ball to figure out where to go. At night Dung Beetles use the Milky Way as a guide to steer the dung ball home.

Scientists have found evidence of Dung Beetles on Earth from as long ago as 30 million years.

The Ninja Bug!
The Assassin Bug

The Assassin Bug stabs through the exoskeleton of its prey using its hardened mouthpart called a rostrum.

It then injects a toxin into the prey, which turns their insides into liquid mush, and kills them. Assassin Bugs eat ants, termites, bees and beetles.

They are no danger to humans, but their bite can be painful. The after effects of the pain can sometimes last for months.

Some Assassin Bugs secrete a sticky substance from their exoskeletons. Some use this to stick and carry their dead prey on their backs. Others stick debris and other garbage onto their backs. They put stuff on their backs to act as camouflage. This also disguises their smell because they take on the smell of whatever is on their backs.

23

24

Weird and Colorful!
The Spiny Flower Mantis

This tiny bug is between 1 to 2 inches long and lives in Southern and Eastern Africa. The Spiny Flower Mantis is the cousin of the better known Praying Mantis.

The adult has spiny structures on the underside of its body, giving it its name. It can be green, yellow, pink or red in color. It has a striking spiral eyespot mark on its front wings, with a round spot in black, green and cream surrounded by a green patch.

When threatened it spreads its front wings, making itself appear bigger and displaying its eyespots to scare away would-be predators. This is called a deimatic display.

While resting this mantis is camouflaged and looks like a flower. Insects try to pollinate what they think is a flower and the mantis grabs them and eats them.

The mantis is able to kill prey several times larger than itself.

Dangerous with a cute face!
The Puss Moth Caterpillar

The Puss Moth Caterpillar is most commonly found in thick forests and woodland areas throughout Europe and across parts of Northern Africa.

This caterpillar is green in color with a dark looking spike sticking out from one end and a colorful "face" on the other.

When threatened the Puss Moth Caterpillar sprays formic acid into the face of its attacker. Because of this it is the most dangerous caterpillar species in Great Britain. Formic acid is often used as a preservative and is also found in bee and ant stings.

Puss Moth Caterpillars live in willow and poplar trees and feed on their leaves. The caterpillars generally remain in an area where there are a number of trees to feast on.

Puss Moth Caterpillars build hard waterproof cocoons. These cocoons are the strongest built among moth species.

27

28

7 MORE STRANGE BUT TRUE BUG FACTS:

1) About 80% of the Earth's animals are insects!

2) A mosquito flaps its wings 500 times a second.

3) Some snails can sleep for 3 years straight!

4) A butterfly has its taste receptors in its feet!

5) The female black widow's poison is 15 times deadlier than a rattlesnake's!

6) There are worms in Australia that are over 4 Feet Long!

7) Cockroaches can survive underwater for up to 15 minutes.

The Champion Hunter!
Dragonflies

Dragonflies are the champion hunters of all animals on Earth.

Lions catch their prey less than 1 in every 4 tries. Great White Sharks do a bit better — 1 in 2 tries. African Wild Dogs are even better — 2 out of every 3 tries. Cougars catch 8 out of every 10, or are 80% successful at capturing their prey.

Dragonflies capture 95 to 97% of the prey they hunt! Super hunters!

Why are Dragonflies such successful hunters? What is their secret?

Dragonflies do not chase their prey. They ambush their prey from behind.

Dragonflies have the best vision in the insect world with a 360 degree view. They can see to the front, left and right, and behind them.

They also have incredible flying abilities in the air. They can move their four wings separately and each wing can be rotated on its own.

Dragonflies catch other flying insects, like midges and mosquitoes.

31

32

I Glow in the Dark!

Fireflies

Fireflies are actually Beetles and not Flies. "Firebeetles" just doesn't sound as good as "Fireflies".

When a chemical called luciferin inside their tail combines with oxygen, calcium and adenosine triphosphate, a chemical reaction occurs that creates their spectacular light.

Firefly light can be yellow, green or orange.

There are more than 2,000 species of fireflies. They are found on all continents other than Antarctica. Only some species produce adults that glow. Fireflies in the Western United States cannot produce light.

Males that do glow use their flash to attract females. Each species has its own pattern of light flashing. In some places at some times, Fireflies flash their light in sync with one another.

The light produced by the Firefly is the most efficient light ever made. Almost 100 percent of the energy in the chemical reaction is emitted as light. A normal light bulb only emits 10 percent of its energy as light, the other 90 percent is lost as heat.

The "You Can't Miss Me" Bug!
The Striped Shieldbug

The Striped Shieldbug is easily identified. It is a black bug with five distinct red lines on its back. On the underside the Striped Shieldbug is red as well, but here it has black spots, not lines.

This bug is known by a few other names — The Italian Striped Bug or the Minstrel Bug.

The bold red and black colors warn predators that this bug is really bad tasting. This helps protect the bug.

Even though it is closely related to the Green Stinkbug and other foul smelling bugs, the Striped Shieldbug smells like apples.

The Striped Shieldbug is found in Europe, North Africa and the Near East.

35

36

The Giant Killer!
The Tarantula Hawk Wasp

Tarantula Hawks are large, long legged wasps which prey on Tarantula Spiders. They are about 2-3 inches long.

They can be found in the Southwestern United States, ranging from California through Arizona, New Mexico, Texas, and as far north as Nevada, Oklahoma and Kansas. The Tarantula Hawk Wasp is also the state insect of New Mexico.

Tarantula Hawks capture and paralyze Tarantula Spiders with their venom. Their stings are the 2nd most painful in the insect world, the Bullet Ant is the most painful.

They then bring the paralyzed spider to an underground nest, lay eggs on the spider and the wasp larvae hatch and feed on the spider.

Adult Tarantula Hawk wasps mostly feed on nectar and they visit flowers and flowering plants during the day.

Despite the fact that they pack a painful punch, this is a non-aggressive insect to humans.

There is no question they are some of the best-defended insects on earth.

In nearly 400 documented battles between Tarantula Hawks and Tarantula Spiders, only once did the Spider win.

Their strong slippery armor allows the wasp to slip away unharmed.

The Super Web Spinner!
Darwin's Bark Spider

Darwin Bark Spiders are found across tropical Africa and Asia. They get their name because some of them look like a bit of bark. This helps to disguise them from predators.

These spiders like to build their webs across bodies of water. Standing on one side of a river or lake, they release a thread of silk into the breeze and it keeps going until it catches onto a twig or leaf on the other side.

Some webs have been measured at 80 feet (25 meters) across. All this from a spider that is less than 1 inch (2.5 cm) long!

The web looks like any other spider web with spokes and spirals. The difference is they just happen to be right above a river or even a lake filled with water. With such a huge span the webs of the Darwin Bark Spiders are the largest spider webs in the world.

These giant webs catch unsuspecting mayflies, damselflies, bees and dragonflies flying over the water.

This spider's silk is the strongest fiber on earth. It is up to 6 times stronger than high-grade steel per weight. Its silk is 10 times stronger than Kevlar, which is used to make bullet proof vests.

It is at least two times tougher than any other spider's silk.

THANKS FOR READING!

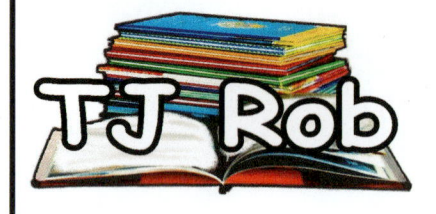

Please leave a review at your favorite bookseller's website - such as Amazon - share with other readers what you liked about this book.

Visit www.TJRob.com for a FREE eBook and to discover TJ Rob's other exciting books

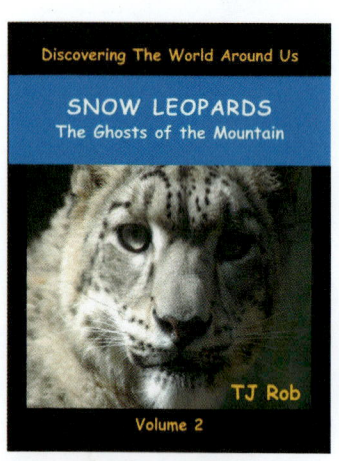

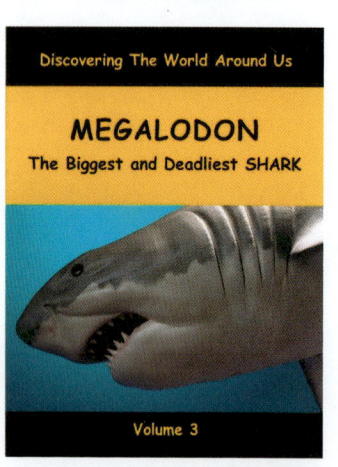

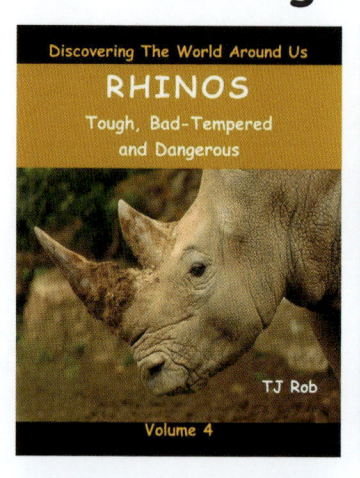

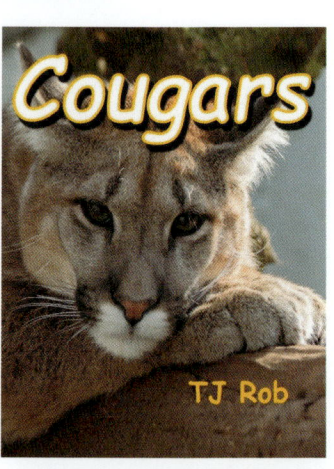

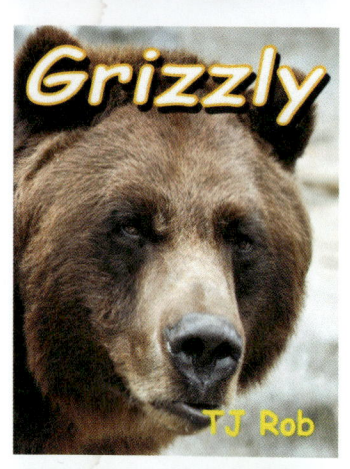

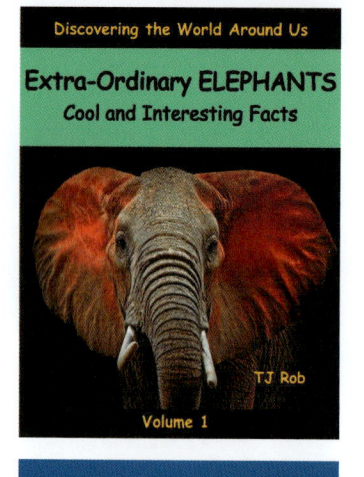

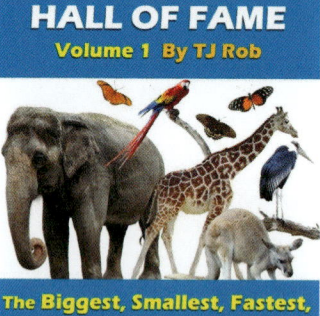

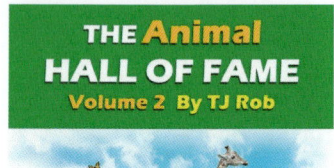

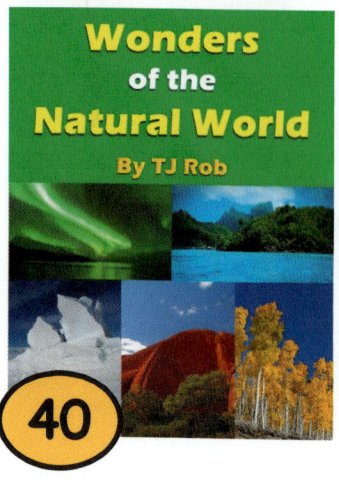

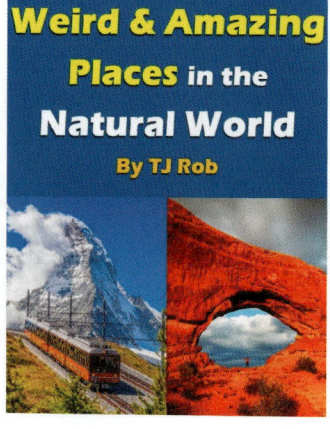

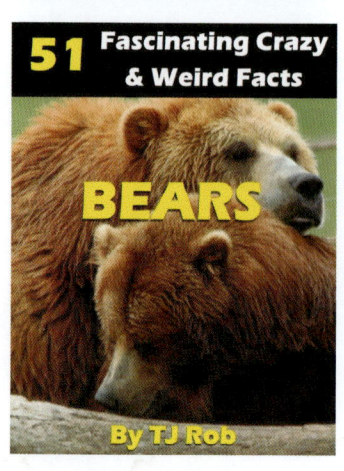

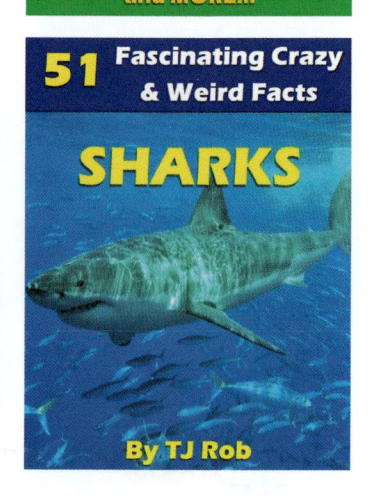

Printed in Great Britain
by Amazon